She...

WRITTEN BY KOBI YAMADA   DESIGNED BY SARAH FORSTER

She must be something special.

SHE IS. CELEBRATE HER.

Who is she? She is simply extraordinary. Not just because of the things she says and does, but because of the spirit and grace with which she does them.

She touches hearts and minds as she goes about her daily life—sometimes not even knowing the difference she makes. She could be someone you've just met or someone you've known forever. But no matter who she is, she adds so much beauty and brilliance to the world.

She LOVES life and it loves her RIGHT BACK.

CELEBRATE HER PASSION.

She listens
TO HER HEART
above all
THE OTHER VOICES.

CELEBRATE HER WISDOM.

She pursues BIG dreams
INSTEAD OF SMALL REALITIES.

CELEBRATE HER PRIORITIES.

She sees every ending as a new beginning.

CELEBRATE HER ENTHUSIASM.

She knows her REAL measurements have NOTHING to do with numbers or statistics.

CELEBRATE HER SELF-ESTEEM.

SHE IS KIND, loving, and patient... with herself.

CELEBRATE HER SPIRIT.

She wakes up each day
and THROWS AWAY her excuses.

CELEBRATE HER ACCOUNTABILITY.

She listens to HER HEAD AS WELL as her heart.

CELEBRATE HER CHOICES.

She
welcomes
unexpected
delights.

CELEBRATE HER SPONTANEITY.

She turns
HER CAN'TS
into cans
AND HER
dreams
INTO PLANS.

CELEBRATE HER GOALS.

She ignores those
who say it CAN'T be done.

CELEBRATE HER RESILIENCE.

She has a way of
TURNING OBSTACLES
into opportunities.

CELEBRATE HER PERSEVERANCE.

She realizes that SHE'S the ONE she's been waiting for.

CELEBRATE HER INDEPENDENCE.

She's strong enough
TO KEEP HER HEART open.

CELEBRATE HER VULNERABILITY.

She makes
the whole world
feel like home.

CELEBRATE HER WARMTH.

She adds
SO MUCH
beauty to
BEING HUMAN.

CELEBRATE HER PRESENCE.

She walks in when EVERYONE ELSE WALKS OUT.

CELEBRATE HER FRIENDSHIP.

She JUST has a
way of brightening
the day.

CELEBRATE HER RADIANCE.

She makes
LIFE FUN.

CELEBRATE HER JOY.

She colors her thoughts with ONLY the BRIGHTEST hues.

CELEBRATE HER OPTIMISM.

She imagines it,
AND THEN SHE
makes it happen.

CELEBRATE HER DETERMINATION.

She's an artist and LIFE IS HER CANVAS.

CELEBRATE HER CREATIVITY.

She runs ahead where
there are no paths.

CELEBRATE HER COURAGE.

SHE LOOKS
the world
STRAIGHT
in the eye.

She fearlessly crosses borders and REFUSES to recognize limits.

CELEBRATE HER CAPABILITIES.

She knows when to hold on
and when to let go.

CELEBRATE HER GRACE.

She NOT ONLY sees a light at the end of the tunnel, she BECOMES that light for others.

CELEBRATE HER COMPASSION.

She lives for
TODAY AND BUILDS
for tomorrow.

CELEBRATE HER POSSIBILITIES.

She remains
TRUE TO HERSELF.

CELEBRATE HER AUTHENTICITY.

She makes the world
a better place.

CELEBRATE HER.

COMPENDIUM®
live inspired

TO HEIDI, SIMPLY MY EVERYTHING. ~K.Y.

WITH SPECIAL THANKS TO THE ENTIRE COMPENDIUM FAMILY.

CREDITS:
WRITTEN BY: KOBI YAMADA
DESIGNED BY: SARAH FORSTER
EDITED BY: NICOLE BURNS ASCUE & AMELIA RIEDLER

LIBRARY OF CONGRESS CONTROL NUMBER: 2015941701
ISBN: 978-1-943200-11-5

2nd printing. Printed in China with soy inks.